O.

The Mystery of Life, Solved by Dessert

Copyright © 2025 Creative Arts Management OÜ

All rights reserved.

Author: Aidan Marlowe
ISBN HARDBACK: 978-1-80566-211-2
ISBN PAPERBACK: 978-1-80566-506-9

Whispers of Confection

In the oven, secrets bake,
Chocolate dreams and velvet flake.
A sprinkle here, a dash of fun,
Life's sweet riddles now weigh a ton.

Bakers laugh at life's great twist,
With every slice, they can't resist.
Flour clouds and icing streams,
Smoothing out our wildest dreams.

Crumbs of Clarity

Cookies tell the tales we hide,
In butter's warmth, we take a ride.
A crunch, a crinkle, then a sigh,
Sweet crumbs whisper why we try.

Sugar lessons often stick,
Even when the clock is thick.
With every nibble, bites of lore,
Unravel secrets, wanting more.

Frosting on the Puzzle

Life's a cake, unfrosted square,
With sprinkles flying everywhere.
We stab the knife, and hope to see,
Layers of truth, wild as can be.

Jokes in frosting, colored bright,
Tricky bites can bring delight.
Each slice brings a giggling cheer,
Solving puzzles year by year.

A Taste of Understanding

Spoonfuls of joy in a sundae cup,
Twists and turns as we scoop it up.
Every flavor sings a tune,
Life's dilemmas vanish soon.

Maraschino cherries on top,
With every layer, we can't stop.
Knowledge hidden in every bite,
Digging deep brings sweet delight.

Candied Curiosities

In a world of sugar and spice,
Where sweet dreams come at a price,
A twist of lemon makes you grin,
Unlocking secrets held within.

When jellybeans start to dance,
They spark a candy-coated romance,
With licorice whips and brownie bites,
To solve life's woes, we take to flights.

Tarts of Time

Time rolls on like flaky crust,
With blueberry filling, it's a must,
Each slice a moment, tart and sweet,
Where memories and pastries meet.

A sprinkle of cinnamon on top,
As laughter rings, we never stop,
Sipping tea while tarts appear,
In every bite, a joy so clear.

Marzipan Mystiques

In almond dreams, the answers lie,
With marzipan creatures flying by,
They whisper truth in sugary tongues,
As giggles burst from everyone young.

With every bite, a secret found,
Life's riddles sweetly dance around,
Wrapped in flavors, bold and bright,
The answers come with each delight.

Gelato Journeys

Scoops of joy on a sunny day,
Taste the rainbow, come what may,
Each swirl a step into the unknown,
Where every cone feels like home-grown.

Chocolate fudge or minty cheer,
The path is paved with ice cream here,
As laughter drips in every drip,
We travel far on dessert's sweet trip.

Sweetness as Sage

With sprinkles of wisdom, I bake my thoughts,
A cherry on top, where confusion rots.
Whisking together my dreams with some cream,
In chocolatey puddles, I plot and I scheme.

Mix folly with flour, let laughter rise high,
As cupcakes debate under icing sky.
Are answers found in a fudge-covered pie?
I'd say that's dessert – oh me, oh my!

Cookies of Contemplation

Nestled in jars, secrets await,
Each cookie a riddle, of sugary fate.
Should I ponder on sprinkles, or bite into bliss?
A peanut butter puzzle, oh how could I miss?

Dunking in milk, my thoughts start to frolic,
In crumbs of wisdom, life's lessons symbolic.
One cookie at a time, I nibble and grin,
Finding meaning at the bottom, let the fun begin!

Morsels of Meaning

In every pie slice, a tale to be told,
Of laughter and joy, and adventures bold.
Bite into the layers, let flavors surprise,
You'll uncover a truth, with sweet little ties.

Marshmallow mysteries, oh so profound,
In every soft layer, new meanings abound.
Why is the cake round? Is life just this sweet?
In crumbs of reflection, I find my heartbeat.

Dessert Dreams

In a world made of sugar, the fanciest sights,
Where tarts are the rulers, and brownies take flights.
I dream of a realm where the frosting stands tall,
Where laughs are the currency, and joy is our call.

So let's raise our spoons to the desserts we adore,
To the marshmallow clouds and the soufflé encore.
For in every celebration, a giggle rings true,
Life's sweetest confessions await me and you!

Sweet Revelations

In a cake, I see my fate,
Frosting smooth, I can't wait.
With each bite, answers come,
Who needs wisdom when there's gum?

Cookies whisper secrets sweet,
Crunchy joy, a tasty treat.
Sprinkles dance, like stars at night,
Life's problems fade with each bite.

Chocolate Whispers

In a bar, they hide away,
All the secrets of the day.
Melting thoughts in creamy swirl,
Who knew craziness could twirl?

Guilty pleasures wrapped in foil,
Thoughts of work, now they uncoil.
With each square, my mind's at ease,
Forget my troubles, say cheese!

Crumbs of Understanding

From a pie, I learn or two,
Life is sweet, and so are you.
Crusty edges, flaky charm,
One more slice could do no harm!

Every crumb tells tales anew,
Of silly dreams and skies so blue.
With a nibble, I start to see,
That dessert holds the key for me.

Layers of Enigma

In trifle's depth, I lose my way,
Every bite, a game to play.
Whipped cream thoughts, so light and airy,
Life's puzzles seem less scary.

Pudding cups with history,
Each layer, a sweet mystery.
Spoon in hand, I dig away,
Solving life, in a sugary ballet.

Sugar-Coated Secrets

In a bowl of dreams, we mix it right,
A sprinkle of sugar, everything's bright.
Whisk away worries, let laughter unfurl,
Desserts hold the answers, in a sweet swirl.

Chocolate may hide what we wish to find,
A crusty old pie with a flaky mind.
Slice up the truth, taste the delight,
Sugar-coated secrets dance in the night.

Slices of Clarity

Cut through the fog with a pie on a plate,
Flavors reveal what our hearts contemplate.
Whipped cream on top gives a silly charm,
In a world of confusion, it keeps us warm.

Strudel or tart, it's all in the slice,
Each bite of joy is a roll of the dice.
Fruit fills the gaps where answers won't flow,
Life's puzzle solved with a sweet, tasty show.

The Cake of Existence

Layers and layers, oh what a feat,
Life's questions hide under frosting so sweet.
Bite into life, let the flavors collide,
With sprinkles of joy, we take it in stride.

Candles a'burning, each wick a new year,
With every sweet slice, we dissolve all fear.
A cherry on top, a vibrant delight,
Cake holds the keys to our sleepless nights.

Frosted Truths

In the frosting we find what we seek in jest,
Whimsical tales where the chaos can rest.
One scoop of laughter, a dollop of fun,
Life's frosted truths shine brighter than sun.

A cookie tells tales with a crunch and a crumble,
Bringing us wisdom before we stumble.
In every pastry, a story we taste,
Frosted truths are too good to waste.

The Truffle Theory

Round and rich, a truffle rolls,
Sweetened secrets, chocolate goals.
Are we just treats, in disguise?
Life's a box of tasty lies?

Crunchy shells and creamy dreams,
A sprinkle here, or so it seems.
With every bite, a laugh we find,
Cocoa wisdom, sweet and kind.

Caramelized Confusion

Sticky situations, what a mess,
Pouring syrup to impress.
A drizzle brightens every frown,
Life's a tangle, spin us 'round!

In the pot, colors swirl and dance,
Like our lives, it's just a chance.
Crispy edges, gooey centers,
Caramel dreams that are true inventors.

Fondant Facets

Layers thick, like life's own cake,
With every slice, a laugh to make.
Fondant smiles, and sugary cheer,
Which sweet shape holds life's true fear?

Crafting joy with a rolling pin,
Smoothing edges, let fun begin.
Life's just frosting, white and swirl,
Underneath, just a plain old world.

Pies that Speak

Oh, the pies that sit and wait,
Whisper secrets on a plate.
Apple grins and cherry winks,
Each slice tells us what life thinks!

With every fork, a tale unfolds,
Of love and laughter, oh so bold.
Pastry crusts, they hold the key,
To solving problems, one, two, three!

Crusty Quandaries

In pie crusts, secrets swirl and bake,
What's hidden in layers of sweet flake?
A cherry giggles, a blueberry sighs,
With every slice, a surprise that multiplies.

Is life like a tart, or a stale old loaf?
Each bite's a riddle, a crumb of hope.
A sprinkle of sugar, a pinch of delight,
Crusty quandaries vanish, just right!

Whisking Away Doubts

Whisk in the bowl, let worries fly,
Eggs and frosting, oh me, oh my!
Doubts dissolve in a creamy blend,
Who knew a cupcake could be my friend?

With sprinkles of laughter, we whip up glee,
Each frosting swirl sets my worries free.
A scoop of this, a dash of that,
Whisking away doubts, imagine that!

Sugary Solutions

The answer to life? It's found in the pie,
With a fork and a grin, give it a try.
Chocolate ganache, or perhaps lemon zest,
Sugary solutions, who knew they'd impress?

When life throws curveballs, just bake it away,
A sprinkle of humor to brighten my day.
In cookies and cream, I find my muse,
Sugary solutions, I cannot refuse!

Flaky Foundations

On flaky foundations, we dance and we bake,
With laughter and crumbs, we stir up the flake.
Pastries and giggles, a whimsical blend,
Each flaky bite brings good vibes to send.

Life's like a croissant, buttery bliss,
Rotate your worries, don't give them a kiss.
With layers of fun, and a sprinkle of zest,
Flaky foundations, feeling truly blessed!

Icing on the Inquiry

In a world where questions abound,
Chocolate frosting is often found.
I ponder deep while cake I eat,
Are sprinkles the answers? Oh, how sweet!

With each bite, I feel so wise,
Cookie crumbs beneath the skies.
If life's a riddle, what's the score?
A scoop of ice cream, I demand more!

Pastries of Perception

Croissants twirl like life's own fate,
Flaky layers, we contemplate.
Do éclairs hold the secrets divine?
Or is it just custard, oh so fine?

Life's questions rise, buttery and warm,
With each pastry, we break the norm.
Pie charts? Nah, we want pie to share!
Sugar-coated truths fill the air.

A Taste of Understanding

What does it mean to truly know?
Perhaps it's in the fudge we stow.
A pie of wisdom, a slice so bright,
Each forkful brings clarity and delight.

Is frosting the glue to make sense of things?
Or just a sugary hope that life sings?
Let's whip up laughter in a bowl,
And savor desserts to feed the soul.

Confections of Clarity

In jellies and jams the answers hide,
Sticky truths we cannot bide.
A gummy bear, a chewy thought,
In this candy shop, wisdom's bought.

With lollipops, the questions spin,
Do marshmallows hold where we begin?
Each bite a joke, each crunch a plea,
Sweet confections, the key to glee!

Whipped Cream Whispers

In a world of fluff and cream,
Where each dollop holds a dream,
A spoonful's spark, a frosting sigh,
Underneath the sugar sky.

With every swirl, a giggle found,
Chocolate rivers dance around,
Who knew a cake could make me grin?
Life's conundrums melt within.

Layers of Intrigue

Between the layers, secrets hide,
Caramel oozes, can't confide.
Each bite a clue, a crumbly trail,
What lies beneath this fluffy veil?

Pineapple, nuts, oh what a mix,
Like a riddle, sweet little tricks.
Piecing together, with every taste,
Life's puzzles gone without a waste.

Sifting Through Sweetness

Flour clouds float in the air,
Sifting through, without a care.
Cookies whisper their sweet delight,
As brownies wink in the soft moonlight.

A sprinkle here, a dash of fun,
Baking's math can't come undone.
Mixing chaos in a bowl,
Frosting dreams are the ultimate goal.

Fruitcake Revelations

Layers of fruit, odd and bizarre,
Rum-soaked wonders, oh, how they spar.
Each slice tells tales of time gone past,
In this cake, traditions last.

With nuts that laugh and spices sing,
The quirkiest joy that desserts bring.
Conversations stir with juicy zest,
Life's secrets hidden, yet expressed.

Comfort in Confections

In a world full of mush, we seek sweet delight,
With chocolate and sprinkles, we welcome the night.
A donut's sweet smile, a cake's gentle grin,
In frosting we find where our joys all begin.

When life gets too salty and troubles arise,
We bake with a spirit that seldom complies.
Cookies dance 'round, with flavors so bold,
In every warm bite, a new tale unfolds.

From Flour to Wisdom

With flour in hand, we ponder and muse,
Mixing in laughter, we pick and we choose.
Brownies and cookies lead us to know,
The answers are sweet, as we stir and we go.

In cakes we confide, with layers to share,
Each bite brings us courage, as life's truths lay bare.
A whisk full of hope, a sprinkle of chance,
In dessert's warm embrace, we twirl and we dance.

Biscuit Beneath the Surface

Beneath the crust lies a tale never told,
Of butter and secrets and truths to behold.
Each biscuit a puzzle, flaky and light,
Craving a crunch, we munch with delight.

Dig deeper we must, for the flavor we seek,
With gravy as gold, we find what we tweak.
So rise with your biscuits, let laughter abound,
In each savory bite, life's wonders are found.

Delicious Dilemmas

Sundae or pie, what a tough call to make,
Each scoop a dilemma, each slice a mistake?
With sprinkles and cherries, we try to decide,
When sweetness is calling, our worries subside.

As forks start to fall, and our laughter will soar,
Our plate holds the answers; who could ask for more?
In sugar we trust, with each playful bite,
Life's quirks seem much clearer, when desserts hold the light.

The Crust Beneath

In the oven, secrets bake,
A sweet disguise, make no mistake.
Crusty edges, flavors tease,
Reveal the truth with every piece.

Whisking cream with joy anew,
Batter spills, but who cares, woo-hoo!
Laughter bubbles in the pan,
Desserts unite the world, oh man!

Sprinkles hide the tales untold,
Sugar's kiss makes dark days bold.
Mixing joy in every scoop,
Happiness is just a spoonful loop.

So when life's puzzles seem too tight,
Take a slice, and feel just right.
Sweets are mapped with laughter's spark,
Unravel life's quirks in the dark.

Between Bites and Beliefs

In every bite, a tale unwinds,
A spoonful of faith, and all's aligned.
Caramel dreams flow without end,
In the kitchen, we find a friend.

Whipped cream clouds, they touch the skies,
Chocolate whispers, oh so sly.
Baking's magic, a twist of fate,
In each dessert, we contemplate.

Crumble fears with buttery crust,
Take a leap, it's a must!
Pastry puzzles, life's little tricks,
Crafting joy with sugar sticks.

Life's oddities, we stir along,
With every taste, we grow more strong.
Between bites, beliefs set sail,
In frosted layers, we unveil.

Savory Solutions

A pie for every question asked,
Golden crust, the truth unmasked.
Berry enchantments, speak so clear,
With every fork, we share a cheer.

Dinner doubts, we let them rest,
Desserts are here; they are the best.
Filling plates with laughter's grace,
Solving woes in sugar's embrace.

Pudding mystery, oh so thick,
Pouring joy in every lick.
Life's big questions, we polish bright,
In decadent layers, we take flight.

So when uncertainties ebb and flow,
Just grab a treat, and let it show.
Savory bites, they laugh and play,
Turn the ordinary into ballet.

Layered Lore

Life's a cake with secrets stacked,
Frosting dreams in layers packed.
Beneath the cream, our stories lie,
With every slice, we reach the sky.

Whispered tales of sugar spun,
Changing views, just add some fun.
Chocolate chips, a twisty fate,
Every bite, a chance to celebrate.

In whipped delight, we find our tune,
Mixing truth beneath the moon.
Giggling spoons and giggly kids,
Sifting through life's truth, like lids.

Layered lore in every bake,
Finding joy in every flake.
So take a taste, don't be shy,
Desserts reveal, oh my, oh my!

Medleys of Meringue

In a world of cream and fluff,
Where sweetness reigns, it's never tough.
A swirl of clouds on a pie plate,
Miracles happen, just don't be late.

Fluffy peaks and golden crust,
Sugar feels like a must.
You take a bite, who needs a clue?
Each morsel's magic, just for you.

Whip it fast, don't let it fall,
The secret's hidden in each call.
A dance of flavors, light and bright,
Who knew fun could fit so tight?

So here's the scoop, or maybe two,
Dessert's a riddle that's always true.
With every bite, a giggle comes,
Life's a jest, and cake's the drums.

Enigmatic Eclairs

Puffs of pastry filled with cheer,
Who can solve what's hidden here?
With chocolate drips and cream inside,
Whispers sweet, it's quite the ride.

Each delicate bite is a quick quest,
Eclairs tease, they never rest.
Mind's a jumble, taste buds lead,
Laughter blooms, it's quite the feed.

They float above on frosting dreams,
With every crunch, joy brightly beams.
What's the secret? Who can say?
Enjoy the surprise, take one today!

So dive right in, chase the thrill,
Each eclair laughter can fulfill.
No answers found? Just savor more,
Life's a treat, not a boring chore.

Cakey Confessions

Between the layers, secrets hide,
Flavors mingle, side by side.
Frosted tales of lemon zest,
Forgive the calories, it's for the best.

With every slice, confessions spill,
Chocolate whispers, oh, what a thrill.
Marziapan moments, all entwined,
Cakey dreams, blissfully blind.

Each dessert tells stories sweet,
Of love and laughter, life's heartbeat.
A fork in hand, we dive right in,
Let the sugary shenanigans begin!

Guilt be gone, in this sweet mess,
Life's enigma, we must confess.
Cakes and joy, a savory pair,
In this conundrum, life's light as air.

Harvesting Happiness

In the garden of treats, we may find,
A crostata that's truly kind.
Fruit and crust—what a delight,
Pie meets laughter, oh what a sight!

Berries burst and flavors dance,
In this mix, we take a chance.
A slice of joy upon each plate,
Happiness served—it's never late.

Crumbles and squirts, oh messy bliss,
Life's too short to be amiss.
Gather sweets like blooms in spring,
Each bite echoes the joy we bring.

So who knew dessert could reveal,
The chuckles hidden, the love we feel?
In every crumble, a smile grows,
Life's puzzles sweeten, as everyone knows.

Candies of Contemplation

In a jar of jellybeans bright,
I ponder choices with delight.
Each flavor, a thought to unwrap,
In sweetness, I find my map.

Licorice twists teach me to bend,
While sour drops find a sweet end.
Fruity bursts make my heart race,
Life's secrets found in candy's embrace.

Pastries of the Profound

Croissants curl with buttery charm,
Each flaky layer, there's no harm.
A scone's crumbliness brings a grin,
In dough, I find where truths begin.

Cream-filled puffs whisper their lore,
Hints of vanilla leave me wanting more.
With every bite, wisdom I gain,
In pastries, I see joy and pain.

Lollipops and Life's Lessons

A lollipop spins with colors bright,
Every lick brings pure delight.
The stickiness teaches me to cling,
To moments that make my heart sing.

With every swirl, a tale unfolds,
Sweet innocence that never gets old.
Round and round like the year's own dance,
Life's lessons wrapped in a sugar trance.

Guilt-Free Indulgence of Truth

In yogurt parfaits, I find my way,
A sprinkle of nuts keeps gloom at bay.
Berries bursting like secrets untold,
In textures and flavors, my truths unfold.

I dive into brownies without a care,
Zero calories? That's a rare affair!
With each scoop of froyo, I smile wide,
Finding joy in the sweetness, my heart's guide.

Frosting on the Soul

Whisk away the blues,
A cupcake in hand,
With sprinkles and giggles,
Life gets unplanned.

Sugar-coated secrets,
Gather round to share,
The frosting's thick layers,
Hide joy everywhere.

Whipped cream laughs softly,
On pies and on tarts,
Dessert is a language,
That speaks to our hearts.

So when life gets rocky,
Just take a sweet bite,
The laughter in flavors,
Makes everything bright.

The Delicate Dance of Dessert

In the kitchen they twirl,
With flour in the air,
Frosting on their faces,
Sweet madness laid bare.

Cupcakes do the cha-cha,
While cookies jive low,
Brownies break out laughing,
Let the sugar flow!

With sprightly delights,
And pie-crust ballet,
Even chocolate puddings,
Join in the fray.

Each bite is a giggle,
A cookie's sly wink,
In this dessert-filled dance,
Life's sweeter than you think.

Whipped Dreams

Dreams float like meringues,
Light, fluffy, and sweet,
In the oven of wonder,
All flavors compete.

Chocolate drips down softly,
Like thoughts we can't keep,
Each scoop is a whisper,
In laughter, we leap.

Pies dance around merrily,
With crusts that can sing,
The joy of confection,
Makes the heart take wing.

So let's whip up our hopes,
In bowls of delight,
Life's dessert-sized dreams,
Are the best kind of bite.

Flavors of Insight

Life's a jar of jelly,
With layers so thick,
Each flavor a lesson,
In the sweetest of tricks.

Marshmallow wisdom,
Fluffy tales untold,
A sprinkle of nutmeg,
Makes the truth feel bold.

So scoop in your laughter,
And serve it with glee,
Dessert gives a glimpse,
Of how fun life can be.

With tart turns of fortune,
And ice cream so bright,
The flavors of wisdom,
Make every wrong right.

Chocolate-Covered Truths

In the land of cocoa dreams,
Sweetness hides behind the seams.
A fudge-filled riddle on my plate,
Unwrap your joys, don't hesitate.

With sprinkles bright, I seek the clue,
Is chocolate love or just fondue?
A brownie whisper, soft and light,
Gives answers wrapped in every bite.

Oh, gooey centers, what do you say?
Life's conundrums melt away.
When in doubt, just take a taste,
Don't let that frosting go to waste!

So grab a fork, let laughter bloom,
In dessert we find the sweet room.
With laughter, cakes, and cookies dear,
You'll find the truth that's crystal clear.

Custard Chronicles

Once in a bowl, smooth and neat,
Custard holds its creamy seat.
Whisking worries 'til they blend,
A tasty tale that has no end.

Each creamy scoop, a story told,
With secret flavors yet untold.
In baked delights, wisdom spills,
Like puddings warm, they cure your ills.

Flavors dance like silly sprites,
Mysteries served in dessert bites.
A spoonful brings a giggle bright,
As we navigate the creamy light.

So gather round, let's munch and talk,
In custard puddles, let's all walk.
For life's conundrums, take a seat,
Discover joy with every treat.

Divine Dilemmas

Sugar-coated questions rise,
In pastries round like perfect pies.
Do I choose the cake or tart?
Decisions made with laughs and heart.

Whipped cream clouds float in the sky,
While sprinkles toss and twirl nearby.
Each sugar rush brings bubbling cheer,
In scrumptious dilemmas, lose your fear.

Crumble or layer, choices abound,
Laughter echoes, happiness found.
In every slice, a riddle spins,
With frosting grace, the fun begins.

Make haste to sample every bite,
When life gets tough, dessert's the light.
So let's indulge, share and delight,
In sugary truths, let's take flight.

Desserted Paths

Along the road where sweets reside,
Desserted paths, let's take a ride.
Through candy canes and chocolate streams,
Life's better wrapped in sugary dreams.

With every step, a cookie crumb,
Each giggle hints, 'You'll overcome!'
Pie-shaped pieces of the whole,
Serve a slice to soothe your soul.

In jello jiggles, wisdom sways,
On frosting hills, we'll laugh and play.
So take the fork, let's dance and dart,
For life's a feast, a work of art.

So tread the paths where cookies roam,
In dessert we find our heart and home.
With every bite, sweet joy ignites,
In laughter's light, our spirit's flights.

Marzipan Musings

In a world where sugar dreams,
Marzipan whispers and giggle beams.
Life's questions fade with every bite,
Chocolate clouds dance in delight.

Frosted secrets in the night,
Sprinkles shining, oh what a sight!
Cakes wearing hats and pies in shoes,
Unwrapping giggles, sweet little clues.

A lollipop's laugh fills the air,
Life's quirks tangled in candied flare.
Every nibble leads to a grin,
And in the laughter, we begin.

So here's to desserts, our joyful guides,
In frosting seas, our doubt subsides.
Life's puzzles melt on the tongue,
In sugary symphonies, we are young.

Cake Walks into the Unknown

A cake once wandered by the moon,
Chasing mysteries, humming a tune.
With frosting boots and a wobbly spin,
Who knew desserts could make us grin?

Whipped cream clouds float overhead,
As donuts giggle in their bed.
Cupcakes juggle with sprinkles bright,
While pie dishes plot their sweet flight.

In ovens deep, secrets are baked,
A cookie's crunch, just what's at stake?
Life's flavors mixed with a chuckle thick,
Sugar-coated jokes make us tick.

So join the cake in its funny quest,
Where desserts shine, and laughter's the best.
With every nibble, we leap and bounce,
In the realm of sweet, life's jokes announce.

Sweets of the Soul

In the pantry of dreams, oh what a scene,
Marshmallow clouds and a jellybean queen.
Life's big questions dressed in pecan pie,
With each scoop smiles reach the sky.

Tart adventures in lemon zest,
Sugar rush, we're feeling blessed.
Gummy bears ponder what to be,
Between fun and frolic, they're never free.

Pudding pots stir with thoughts so neat,
As we unravel each tasty treat.
Sprinkled moments in taffy delight,
Sweet confessions under the starlight.

So savor the laughter, crush your fears,
With desserts nearby, let's shift gears.
In every flavor, we find our role,
Together we dance, the sweets of the soul.

Meringue Mysteries

Once upon a time, light as air,
Meringue floated without a care.
Whispering secrets with each soft sigh,
In a swirl of sweetness, who knows why?

Floating high, where the frosting roams,
A curious dessert searching for homes.
With every twirl, a giggle reveals,
Life's riddles cracked in sugar reels.

A pie in the sky, a tart on the run,
Doughnut detectives seeking fun.
Laughter's the answer, a sprinkle of joy,
In sugary tales, both girl and boy.

So raise your forks to the whims of fate,
Where meringue spins, it's never too late.
With laughter and sweetness, we find our way,
In the mysteries told, we dance and play.

A Sweet Revelation

In a bowl of cream and cheese,
I pondered truths with ease.
Whipped into the perfect fluff,
Each bite says, life's just enough.

Chocolate sprinkles on my nose,
Forget your worries, let life doze.
Every cookie holds a tale,
Of dreams and laughter, let's set sail.

Caramel rivers, oh so gooey,
Life's puzzles seem less screwy.
With pastry lips and sugary grins,
I find the joy where laughter begins.

In frosting swirls, I find the way,
To make the mundane, a brighter day.
Oh, what secrets cakes might keep,
In flour dreams, we'll laugh and leap.

Pudding Portraits

Each pudding cup's a canvas bright,
Stirring my thoughts, oh what a sight!
With cherry smiles and whipped delight,
Life's a joke, just spoon it right.

Banana splits tell tales undone,
Of missed romantic, chocolatey fun.
Swirls of fudge that steal the show,
Who knew happiness could flow so slow?

Crème brûlée, with a crunchy crown,
Life's just cracking, never a frown.
Scoop by scoop, I savor the jest,
In every dessert, I feel so blessed.

So grab your spoons, let's paint the night,
With spoons of joy and sheer delight.
In pots of pudding, secrets hide,
Join the feast, there's nothing to bide.

Sweet Enigmas of Existence

A pie says life is just a slice,
Serve it warm, oh, isn't it nice?
With berries bursting, oh what fun,
In every bite, a riddle spun.

Cupcakes whisper sweet, soft tales,
With frosting waves and sugary sails.
Each sprinkle a plan, goofy and bright,
Takes the edge off, makes it just right.

Sundaes hold secrets, tall and grand,
With whipped cream waves that clearly stand.
As I dig in, I give a cheer,
For in each layer, happiness near.

So let's uncover each sugary clue,
In desserts, life's wonders brew.
The answers swirl, all intertwined,
In the laughter shared, the joy defined.

Sugar-Coated Secrets

Cookies hide smiles in every batch,
As we chew them, life's a match.
Chocolate chips, like stars at night,
Illuminating paths of sheer delight.

Jelly-filled doughnuts, secrets inside,
Bite through the sweetness, take a ride.
Every glaze holds a whimsy spark,
In each crumb, the joy leaves a mark.

Brownies reflect the depth we crave,
A fudgy answer, oh how we wave!
With every edge that we delight,
Life's simple puzzles come to light.

Let's toast with spoons, a sugar cheer,
Life's not so hard with desserts near.
In every forkful, laughter's found,
In treats and giggles, life astounds.

Tasty Epiphanies

In the kitchen, chaos reigns,
Flour flies, like in a plane.
But a cake emerges, wondrous sight,
Sweet satisfaction feels so right.

Frosting rivers, sugar hills,
Chocolate rivers cure all ills.
As I nibble, ideas bloom,
Life's perplexities meet their doom.

Sprinkles dance, a wild flair,
Each bite whispers, 'Have no care.'
A cupcake giggles, soft and round,
In each morsel, joy is found.

From pies to tarts, a smiling face,
Desserts bring comfort, a warm embrace.
When problems rise, I turn to bake,
In every bite, a sweet mistake.

A Spoonful of Wonder

A spoonful here, a sprinkle there,
Mixing laughter, love, and flair.
Ice cream mountains, syrup seas,
Life's big questions melt with ease.

Baking cookies, crispy fun,
Each batch says, 'You've already won!'
Doughy secrets, floured dreams,
Life's absurdity in whipped cream themes.

Spoons collide with joyful sounds,
In every scoop, a truth abounds.
Pudding mysteries float anew,
Dessert reveals what's false and true.

With each bite, laughter swells,
Finding answers in cake's sweet spells.
A scoop of joy, a dash of wow,
Desserts teach wisdom, here and now.

The Puzzle of Pastry

Crusts and toppings, a flaky quest,
Every pastry hides a jest.
Tarts and layers, oh so grand,
Each dessert has a secret plan.

Pies with fillings, mystery sweet,
Life's questions resolve with each treat.
Whisking worries into the air,
With a pie slice, I'm free of care.

Slicing layers, like life's own maze,
Every bite's a funny craze.
From éclairs to cookies, giggles burst,
In dessert we trust, for better or worse.

A doughnut's hole shows what's amiss,
In treats so small, find infinite bliss.
Life's puzzles solved with sugary grace,
A pastry masterpiece in every place.

Confectionary Questions

What's the meaning of a chocolate cake?
A slice of joy for goodness' sake.
Gummy bears giggle, jelly beans cheer,
Every treat whispers, 'Life's not so severe.'

Lollipops twirl in shimmering light,
Candy corn dances, oh what a sight!
In the realm of sweets, dilemmas fade,
Life's heavy thoughts mischaracterized by tirade.

Marshmallow dreams float in the sky,
Fudge thinks deeply, as cupcakes sigh.
Dessert debates are a curious thing,
In every confection, the joy they bring.

So here's to pastries, treats galore,
To every question, there's one more.
With every nibble, find what's true,
In boundless sweets, our laughter grew.

Sweets of Suspense

In shadows we ponder, sweet or not,
A cupcake whispers secrets, a muffin plots.
Chocolate chips giggle, frosting's delight,
Will dessert save the day, or just tease our bite?

They sit on the counter, vibrant and bright,
Caramel tales told in the dead of night.
With every good scoop, the tension does rise,
As sprinkles of laughter dance under the skies.

A cookie's great wisdom, so chewy and bold,
Tells stories of pastry, both new and old.
Yet beneath the glaze, those mysteries hide,
What joy truly means, oh, how deep they abide!

So grab that fork swiftly, just dive right in,
For the truth lies in sweets, and with guilt comes the win.
Let's solve life's enigma, one dessert at a time,
With chocolate as the answer, the world feels sublime.

Crème Brûlée Philosophy

A torch in hand, a caramel crust,
What wisdom it brings, led by trust.
A crack, then the shine, the dream we pursue,
In each golden layer, there's something quite new.

Philosophers ponder, as they dig with a spoon,
Is this the sweet spark that'll lead to the moon?
Or just custard mischief, hiding under charms,
With every soft scoop, it whispers 'no harms.'

Glancing at options, a pastry case wide,
What if love's like chocolate that melts and can't hide?
A dessert's reflection of life's big parade,
With custard in hand, let the debates be laid.

Enjoy the sweet chaos, embrace every bite,
For answers may lurk, but laughter is bright.
In desserts, we find joy, and flavors so sage,
Crème brûlée musings will always engage.

Unraveling in Raspberry

A berry so bold, red jewels on a plate,
Its tangy allure is a playful fate.
Life's puzzles unravel with a sprinkle or two,
As raspberry whispers, 'Join in for the view.'

Jams of confusion, on toast they reside,
Is it breakfast or dessert? We pick a side.
The tartness of wisdom, in sweetness concealed,\nLife's
riddles dissolve when dessert is revealed.

Each spoonful a giggle, a tart little jest,
Hidden truths melt away at the dessert fest.
With whipped cream atop, and maybe some pie,
Life's answers are silly, and we can't deny.

So here's to the berry, vibrant and spry,
Its laughter spills over, oh my, oh my.
Sweets bring us closer, to what we seek most,
In raspberry's glow, we'll laugh and we'll toast!

Dessert Dialogues

In the bakery booth, sweet rumbles abound,
Cookies and pastries in dialogue found.
'What's the meaning of life?' asks the warm éclair,
'The icing,' replies cake, 'is what shows we care.'

A layer of sponge laughs and sings a tune,
'Life's too short, so let's start with the spoon!'
Donuts roll their eyes, 'Don't overthink this!'
'Just dive in,' they cheer, 'and embrace every bliss!'

Mousse teases tart, 'You think you are smart?
But it's all about balance; don't fall apart!'
With each sweet exchange, wisdom they boast,
Life's answers are found in the frosting we toast.

So gather your sweets, let the chit-chat flow,
For pastries and giggles, come join the show.
With humor and buttercream, life's puzzles are clear,
In dessert dialogues, the laughter we hear!

Creamy Conundrums

Whipped cream clouds in a fluffy dome,
Life's big questions stir like ice cream foam.
Mixing flavors, thoughts swirl in a dance,
Slicing through confusion with a tasty glance.

Chocolate fudge, so rich and thick,
Unraveling puzzles, a sweet little trick.
Laughter erupts as sprinkles take flight,
Decoding the universe, one bite at night.

Pie crust crumbles, a sweet little mess,
Even the wise can't always guess.
But with each bite, the answers we seek,
Are layered in laughter, not just technique.

So grab your fork, let's dig in deep,
In dessert we trust — and secrets we keep.
For who knew that frosting held life's grand scheme?
With giggles and crumbs, we frolic and dream.

Carrot Cake Contemplation

In the garden of thoughts, a carrot grows bright,
Twirling around, it shows its delight.
Baked with spices, it whispers so sweet,
Answers to puzzles, in layers they meet.

Chop up your worries, add cream cheese on top,
Savoring bites, let the confusion stop.
Glistening raisins, with nuts all around,
In the batter of laughter, wisdom is found.

With every forkful, the truth starts to gleam,
Life's many riddles unravel like a dream.
So take a big slice, don't hesitate,
In this sweet banquet, we celebrate fate.

As crumbs litter plate, like thoughts in my head,
I laugh at the paths these pastries have led.
For answers lie somewhere, I must confess,
In yumminess wrapped, life's delicious mess.

Tart Temptations

Zesty and bright, the tarts draw me near,
Each fruity filling, a riddle to cheer.
Lemon and berry, they sing with delight,
While pondering questions that dance in the night.

I nibble on crust that crumbles with glee,
With each juicy bite, it sets my mind free.
What's the meaning? Is it peach or is plum?
In this tart riddle, we all feel so dumb.

But laughter erupts over forks and some cream,
Debating the toppings, we twirl in a dream.
With every fresh slice, new ideas take flight,
In the pastry of puzzlement, we savor the night.

So let's toss our troubles into the mix,
Pour love and sugar, through giggles and tricks.
For life's conundrums are sweetly entwined,
In the zest of existence, we often find.

Frosted Fantasies

A swirl of frosting, like clouds in the sky,
Hiding sweet secrets that make spirits fly.
Cakes stacked up high with a whimsical flair,
Delivering giggles as we share what we dare.

With color and sprinkles, our worries grow small,
Life feels more breezy, like a grand carnival.
What does it mean? Just icing, you say,
But life's true flavors come out in the play.

Bittersweet chocolate, it's extra divine,
Fluffing up thoughts with a creamy design.
Every slice cuts through, a sweet little laugh,
In sugared confusion, we dance on its path.

So grab a fork, let's uncover the fun,
Chasing our crumbs till the last bite is done.
For in frosted fantasies, we twirl and we feast,
Where humor and dessert make life a grand feast.

Delights in the Shadows

In the dark of night, I hear a whimper,
A cupcake calling, my heart starts to simper.
Cookies giggle as they sneak away,
Belly laughs rise, come join the play.

Muffins mumble secrets, soft and sweet,
Beneath the table, a sneaky retreat.
Brownies whisper tales of gooey delight,
As spoons dance wildly in the moonlight.

Pies tell stories of fruit all aglow,
Crusts crack jokes only bakers know.
In every slice, a riddle awaits,
Laughter erupts as dough tempts the fates.

With every spoonful, wisdom takes flight,
In the shadows of dessert, everything feels right.
Life's questions dissolve in sugar and cream,
Making it all just one big sweet dream.

Cherry Blossoms and Answers

Under cherry trees, where petals collide,
The fruity delights that warm your inside.
Life's puzzling moments, like pie on a whisk,
With every bite taken, you know what to risk.

Ice cream cones swirl with colorful thoughts,
Banana nut bread, calming all frights.
Whipped cream laughter floats up to the skies,
As donuts debate why the sprinkles aren't pies.

Cake layers whisper, "What's time anyway?"
With frosting that sings, we giggle and sway.
In this garden of flavors, oh what a sight,
Each cherry that falls brings a chance to feel light.

So dive into slices, explore every taste,
For questions dissolve, and troubles should haste.
With every dessert comes a curious crack,
Life's finest secrets—just enjoy the snack!

Chocolate Dreams Unveiled

In the land of cacao, dreams take a stroll,
With truffles and ganache, they play a sweet role.
Life's questions melt under chocolate moonlight,
Fudge-covered wisdom is always in sight.

Brownies debate fraction versus whole cake,
As bonbons frolic, each tasty mistake.
Life's puzzles unravel with every rich bite,
Even the crumbs lead to answers all night.

Chocolate rivers flow with laughter and cheer,
While caramel whispers, "Oh come, have no fear."
Sundaes shout secrets as they bubble and swirl,
In a world filled with sweetness, watch flavors unfurl.

So take a big scoop, let your worries take flight,
In chocolatey realms, everything feels right.
Here, joy is abundant, layered, and bold,
With dessert as the map, let the tales be told.

Biscotti Beneath the Stars

Under the night sky, where dreams are brewed,
Biscotti crunch softly, as tales are imbued.
Each dip in the coffee is a laugh shared anew,
With espresso whispers, life feels like a brew.

Sipping slow wonders while cookies align,
Every crumb holds a secret that's simply divine.
Sweet almond breezes, they giggle and shout,
As sugar-laden mysteries start to sprout.

Stars wink above while confections discuss,
How to enjoy life, how to laugh, and thus.
In every bite of biscotti, joy blooms,
Turning our evenings to whimsical rooms.

So gather your sweets under the starry dome,
With every baked treasure, we're never alone.
For in dessert we find, life's charming delight,
In crumbs and in laughter, we chase through the night.

Tarts of Transcendence

In a world of cake and cream,
Tarts arise, a sweetened dream.
With every bite, the secrets spill,
Sugar-coated, hearts they thrill.

Crusty edges, filling divine,
Mysteries fade with every line.
Whisking joy, we laugh and cheer,
A pastry path, our truth's doth clear.

Blueberries whisper, chocolates shout,
In this dessert, there's no room for doubt.
Life's puzzles melt away like frost,
In pie-filled bliss, we find what's lost.

Join the quest for flaky fun,
As confections shine beneath the sun.
With each dessert, our troubles cease,
Tarts of transcendence bring us peace.

Unraveling with a Spoon

Grab the spoon, it's time to dive,
In puddings rich, let the laughter thrive.
Gelatin jiggles, cakes can't wait,
Unraveling truths upon our plate.

Scoops of joy, a sprinkle of fate,
Each creamy layer relates our state.
With every swirl, we ponder and think,
Spoonfuls of wisdom with a wink.

Chocolate mousse, oh so sly,
Whispering secrets as we scoff and sigh.
Together we munch, in glee we swoon,
Life's puzzles solved with each silver spoon.

Beneath the fluff, conundrums lie,
With every desert, we reach for the sky.
The answers are sweet, don't be a buffoon,
Unraveling the world with a spoon.

Desserts of Destiny

Layered cakes, stacked high with might,
Fate's found in frosting, oh what a sight.
With sprinkles on top, we dare to believe,
In this sugary realm, we boldly cleave.

Fruits parade, colors vibrant and loud,
Each forkful shared, we gather a crowd.
Pies of fortune and tarts of chance,
In dessert's embrace, we swirl and dance.

Life's riddles vanish in whipped cream waves,
Each slice we take, our spirit saves.
The pastries call us, saying come near,
Desserts of destiny, nothing to fear.

Gather 'round, let the feasting commence,
With laughter and joy, and a sweet pretense.
In every dessert, our futures align,
Savor the moments, we're feeling divine.

Savoring the Unseen

In shadows lurk the treats we crave,
Savor the magic, be bold, be brave.
Beneath the crust, a story unfolds,
With every bite, a treasure of golds.

Muffins grinning, their tops all askew,
Whispering secrets of the night's debut.
In every crumb, a tale we find,
Life's quirks and joys, perfectly entwined.

The frosting swirls, a mystic ride,
Cupcakes giggle, never to hide.
A pinch of laughter, a dash of cheer,
Savoring the unseen, oh, rear your ear.

So lift your fork and dig right in,
To laughter and sweetness, let the fun begin.
In every dessert, a riddle takes aim,
Savor the unseen, we share the same game.

Signposts in Sugar

In a world of frosted paths,
Baked goods lead the way.
Muffin maps and candied trails,
Guide the curious stray.

With spoonfuls of whipped cream,
We navigate our dreams.
Gummy bears and pie-shaped stars,
Open up the seams.

Chocolate rivers flow with thought,
Caramel clouds above.
Each bite a gleeful question,
Each crumble speaks of love.

So grab a slice of wisdom,
And savor every taste.
For answers lie in pastries,
No crumb shall go to waste.

Indulgences of Inquiry

Questions rise like dough,
Flour dust upon the cheek.
Each nibble brings new answers,
Though our tummies squeak.

Cakes of contemplation,
Frosted with details sweet.
In the layers of confusion,
We find the perfect treat.

Cookies crack with laughter,
Brownies wink and nod.
Scones come with a riddle,
Life's a frothy façade.

So ponder as you munch,
Explore what each bite shows.
For who needs deep solutions,
When dessert is how it goes?

Pastry Parables

Every tart tells a secret,
Baked to perfection's tune.
Pies of wisdom sit and wait,
Like shadows of the moon.

In the oven's warm embrace,
Philosophy takes shape.
Eclairs filled with wonder,
Where pastry dreams escape.

Donuts full of questions,
Sprinkles of delight.
Sifting through the dough of life,
With each sugary bite.

So laugh and slice the cake,
Share the frosting spread.
For answers lie in sweetness,
In the treats we've all bred.

Trifles of Enlightenment

A scoop of ice cream wisdom,
Melting in the sun.
Cupcakes hold the answers,
When we're just here for fun.

Each bite a celebration,
Of questions big and small.
With jelly beans and pastries,
We giggle through it all.

Tarts of tangy insight,
Cake pops cheer the day.
We'll ponder over pie crusts,
As calories drift away.

So indulge in sweet ensemble,
And let your worries flee.
For life's a grand dessert feast,
So grab your fork with glee!

Macarons and Musings

In lovely hues they dance and play,
A bite of sunshine, bright as day.
With every crunch, a giggle flows,
What secrets lie in those sweet toes?

An almond shell, so crisp and neat,
What's life without a sugary treat?
I ponder deep with every nibble,
Could sugar solve a riddle's scribble?

Meringue swirls, a cloud of glee,
Is joy just whipped up carefully?
As colors mix in playful spins,
I find my truth 'neath frosted skins.

Each bite's a wink, a chuckle shared,
In this dessert, I feel prepared.
To tackle life and all its whims,
With macarons and joyful hymns.

The Solace of Sugar

A cupcake whispers, 'Life ain't bad,'
With sprinkles bright, it makes me glad.
Frosting swirls like dreams untold,
Each bite reveals a joy so bold.

A slice of cake, so rich and fine,
In layers deep, I feel divine.
With every forkful, laughter flows,
What's in the batter? Nobody knows!

Sugar's song is sweet and clear,
A scoop of fun, let's all draw near.
Life's puzzles fade with every taste,
In frosting decadence, we're embraced.

A sprinkle here, a drizzle there,
What's hidden under all that flair?
In every treat, a clue is found,
To life's great joke, we nibble round.

Pies Full of Purpose

A crusty shield, a fruity heart,
What truths unfold with every tart?
Blueberry bursts like wishes blown,
In pastry pockets, secrets grown.

Slice it up, share it wide,
In flaky layers, dreams abide.
Each forkful brings a giggle or two,
At the heart of pie, there's always glue.

Lemon zests and sugar swirls,
In a world of pie, life unfurls.
Do cherries grin, or do they sigh?
With every bite, we dare to try.

The oven hums a merry tune,
While crusts rise beneath the moon.
What purpose lies in a pie so grand?
With laughter and crumbs strewn across the land.

Crusts and Questions

In each flaky crust, a riddle hides,
What sweetness lingers, what joy abides?
An apple's tale, a sprinkle of spice,
Could pie be the answer, oh isn't that nice?

With every bite, I raise a brow,
Is life a puzzle? Tell me how!
A bite of berry, a cheeky grin,
What do we uncover, where do we begin?

A buttery edge, golden and crisp,
Is that a secret of joy we risk?
With every crust and filling divine,
What wisdom waits in dessert's design?

So let's slice into the great unknown,
With laughter and crumbs, together we've grown.
In every tart, a question's thrill,
What's life without dessert? Pure joy, for real!